Beastly Birds and Bats

Lynn Huggins-Cooper

QEB
QEB Publishing

Published in the United States by
QEB Publishing, Inc.
3 Wrigley, Suite A
Irvine, CA 92618

www.qed-publishing.co.uk

Library of Congress Control Number: 2008011766

ISBN 978 1 59566 851 6

Author: Lynn Huggins-Cooper
Edited, designed, and picture researched by:
 Starry Dog Books Ltd.
Consultant: Sally Morgan

Printed in China

Picture credits
Key: t = top, b = bottom, l = left, r = right, c = center,
FC = front cover, BC = back cover.

BSP = Big Stock Photo.com, C = Corbis, D = Dreamstime.com,
F = Fotolibra.com, G = Getty Images, ISP = iStockphoto.com,
M = Morguefile.com, NPL = Nature Picture Library (naturepl.com),
P = Photolibrary, S = Shutterstock.com, SDB = Starry Dog Books.

1 ISP/ © Mark Higgins; 2–3 S/ © Arlene Jean Gee; 4t C/ © Craig Aurness, 4b S/ © iDesign; 5 S/ © Philip Date; 6t ISP/ © Marshall Bruce, 6b C/ © Winfried Wisniewski/zefa; 7 C/ © Peter Johnson; 8–9 C/ © Joe McDonald; 9t ISP/ © Daniel Cardiff, 9b © Art Segal; 10t S/ © Michael Ransburg, 10b ISP/ © Susan Flashman; 11 NPL / © Simon Wagen / J. Downer Product; 12bl S/ © Diego Cervo, 12br M/ sillypieces, 12–13 G/ © Roine Magnusson, 13b C/ © Roger Tidman; 14t P/ © Juniors Bildarchiv, 14b S/ © Rudolf Kotulán; 15 S/ © Andy Z; 16bl ISP/ © David T. Gomez, 16–17 ISP/ © Paul Tessier; 17tr C/ © Michael & Patricia Fogden; 18t C/ © Gary Bell/zefa, 18b S/ © Lori Froeb; 19 ISP/ © Mark Higgins; 20t F/ © Linda Wright, 20b P/ © Friedemann Koster; 21 G/ © Roger Powell/ Foto Natura; 22t C/ © Kit Kittle, 22bl D/ © Argument; 22–23 G/ © Eric Rorer; 23 C/ © Hans Dieter Brandl; Frank Lane Picture Agency; 24t C/ © W. Perry Conway, 24b Professor Phil Myers; 25 C/ © Gary Braasch; 26t © Dr John P. Dumbacher, 26b P/ © Juniors Bildarchiv; 27 © Dr John P. Dumbacher; 29 SDB/ © Nick Leggett.

Contents

Freaky flyers

The world is full of amazing birds. They come in all shapes and sizes, from tiny wrens and hummingbirds to huge birds of prey. Birds are not the only animals that fly. Bats and insects fly, too. We will also look at some strange-looking bats.

▲ *Many birds carry food to their young in their stomach. They **regurgitate** the food for the young to eat.*

▼ *While feeding from flowers, hummingbirds hover in mid-air. Most **species** do this by flapping their wings about 50 times per second.*

All shapes of beaks

Some birds have developed special features and habits for survival. Ducks, for example, have paddle-shaped beaks to help them sieve food from the water. Hummingbirds have long, pointed beaks that they poke deep into flowers so they can drink the **nectar**.

Horrid habits

Birds have many habits that we might think of as unpleasant. These include feeding their young with regurgitated food. Some bats have horrid habits, too. The vampire bat drinks the blood of living creatures. Fruit bats, or flying foxes, like sweet, juicy fruit, just like we do! They can be very large, with a wingspan of 5 feet (1.5 meters).

▲ *After feeding on fruit, the fruit bat licks its claws clean.*

Foul feeders

Birds, such as vultures, eat **carrion**. Turkey vultures sometimes regurgitate what they have eaten because the smell of rotting food puts off **predators**. Other birds regurgitate food to feed their young.

▲ *The hoatzin cannot fly well. It spends a lot of time perching as it digests its meal, making it vulnerable to predators, such as monkeys.*

Hoatzin

The hoatzin, or "stinky cowbird," is a South American cuckoo that smells of cow manure! It uses **bacteria** to **ferment** plant materials in the front part of its gut. This helps the bird to digest its food. The smell is strong enough to put off predators.

Gannets

Gannets are seabirds. They eat large amounts of fish, such as pilchards, anchovies, and squid. Gannets often regurgitate the contents of their stomach if they are disturbed or alarmed.

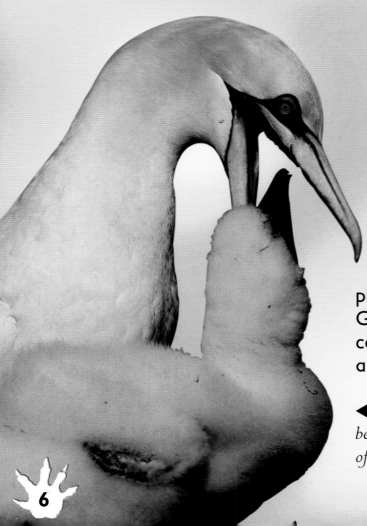

◄ *A baby gannet will tap its mother's beak to get her to regurgitate a meal of partially digested fish.*

Vultures

Vultures are **scavengers**—they eat the remains of dead animals that have been killed by predators, such as lions. Groups of vultures fly in circles above a dying animal, knowing that they will soon have a feast. Vultures have amazingly strong acid in their stomach to help them digest food. Some vultures can even digest bones.

Foul fact!

Most vultures have a bald head. Feathers would be difficult to keep clean as the birds feed on carcasses.

◀ *Different species of vulture feed on the same carcass at different times. White-headed vultures rip open the carcass, white-backed vultures (shown here) eat the insides, and lappet-faced vultures finish off the tough leftovers.*

Putrid pellets

Many larger birds, such as owls and birds of prey, hunt small animals and birds. They gulp down their prey whole, but cannot digest bones, feathers, or fur. These tough parts form pellets that the birds cough up and leave on the forest floor.

Peregrine falcon

The peregrine falcon hunts other birds. It flies over open ground and hedges to flush out its prey, and then swoops. Having caught a bird, the falcon takes it to a "plucking post," such as a tree stump, and pulls out the bird's feathers before eating the rest.

▼ *The peregrine falcon eats the head, feet, intestines, and most of the bones of its prey.*

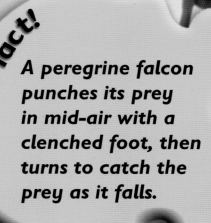

Foul fact!

A peregrine falcon punches its prey in mid-air with a clenched foot, then turns to catch the prey as it falls.

Red-tailed hawk

The red-tailed hawk eats mice, squirrels, rabbits, and other birds. It watches for prey from a perch, and then swoops down, sometimes flying low and chasing its **quarry** across the ground. The red-tailed hawk eats all of its prey, regurgitating the parts that it cannot digest in small pellets.

◄ The red-tailed hawk has long, broad wings, which help it soar through the air.

Owls

Part of an owl's stomach is called the **gizzard**. Here, the fur, bones, and other indigestible parts of its prey are squashed into a pellet. The stored pellet stops the owl from feeding again, so the owl coughs up or regurgitates the pellet.

► If you pull an owl's pellet apart, you can see the tiny bones of the bird's prey.

Dirty defences

Birds need to defend themselves from the many predators, including other birds, that hunt them. They have developed many different ways to do this, some of which are quite unpleasant!

▲ *The northern shoveler has a long, spoon-shaped bill for **filter-feeding** from the water. Its webbed feet help it to swim.*

Northern shoveler

The northern shoveler is a **dabbling duck**. It breeds in wetlands across much of North America, northern Europe, and Asia. If disturbed by a predator, the female shoveler sprays foul-smelling **feces** over her eggs to put the predator off eating them.

Foul fact!

The giant petrel is also known as a "stinker" due to the foul-smelling oil that it vomits at predators!

Petrels

Petrels feed on crabs and fish. Giant petrels also eat **krill**, squid, dead seals, and dead penguins. Their stomach contains a thick, strong-smelling oil that they vomit at intruders. The oil makes feathers less waterproof, so it is dangerous for other birds.

◀ *The petrel makes its nest in pebble-lined rock crevices.*

Fulmars

If an intruder approaches a fulmar's nest, the fulmar makes a coughing noise and then spits oil at the attacker. Even fulmar chicks can do this. Very young chicks can spit small amounts of oil as soon as they leave the egg. By the time they are four days old, they can fire oil a distance of 12 inches (30 centimeters). The chicks may have learned to do this because they are left alone in the nest for long periods while their parents hunt for food at sea.

▼ *The fulmar lays its egg on a grassy cliff edge. Once the chick is about two weeks old, the adult birds leave the nest to search for food.*

▲ *Fulmar chicks use their spitting skills to defend themselves against feral cats, otters, skuas, crows, and gulls.*

Bully boys

Birds can be vicious, both to other birds and to humans. Some birds attack other birds to kill and eat them. Some fight other birds to steal the food they have caught. Some attack to protect their chicks.

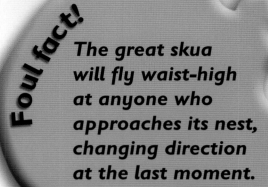

Foul fact! *The great skua will fly waist-high at anyone who approaches its nest, changing direction at the last moment.*

Great skua

The great skua is an aggressive bird with a wingspan of about 4.5 feet (1.4 meters). Some people call it the pirate of the seas. It attacks other birds and steals their prey, and kills and eats puffins and kittiwakes. Skuas also eat fish, **lemmings**, and the eggs and young of other birds.

Magpies

Magpies are common birds often seen in the United Kingdom and Australia. They attack and eat the eggs and young of other birds, including chickens, and are often shot as **vermin** by farmers. The Australian magpie is a particularly aggressive species. A survey found that nine out of ten Australian men had been attacked by a magpie at some time in their lives!

◀ *Male Australian magpies often attack people on bikes, who they may see as being a threat to their newly hatched chicks.*

▼ *The great skua makes harsh screams or barks when attacking intruders.*

Cuckoos

Many types of cuckoo have a bullying habit. The common cuckoo, for example, lays an egg in the nest of a smaller bird. The cuckoo's egg hatches first, and the small bird feeds the young cuckoo, which grows quickly. The cuckoo soon pushes the eggs or chicks of the smaller bird out of the nest.

▶ *The young cuckoo is much bigger than the adult foster bird.*

13

Scavengers

Lots of birds find their food by scavenging. They may eat parts of carcasses left behind by other animals, or they may scavenge for food on garbage tips. Whichever they choose, it can be a messy business.

▲ *The carrion crow's beak is thick and has a curved tip, ideal for picking up and carrying eggs.*

Carrion crow

The carrion crow is a large, black bird that likes to sit on the top of isolated trees so it can spy on the surrounding countryside. It watches birds building their nests, and later attacks them, eating their eggs and young.

Crested caracara

The crested caracara, or Mexican eagle, is the national bird of Mexico. It prefers to eat carrion in the form of dead and rotting fish, or roadkill. Sometimes it will attack brown pelicans and force them to **disgorge** the fish they have caught.

◀ *The male caracara often acts as a lookout, watching for danger from a perch near its nest, to protect its young.*

Marabou stork

The marabou stork is a large bird. Its wingspan can reach a huge 10.5 feet (3.2 meters)—the largest wingspan of any land bird, matched only by the Andean condor. The marabou stork scavenges on carrion and scraps. This may sound unpleasant, but it helps prevent the spread of diseases.

Foul fact!

Marabou storks march in front of grass fires, snatching and eating the small animals that are fleeing.

▶ *The marabou stork's featherless head and neck are easy to keep clean as it feeds.*

Bizarre birds

Some birds look as if they have been put together using the different parts of other birds! From birds with strange beaks to birds with peculiar habits, there are some very bizarre birds in the world.

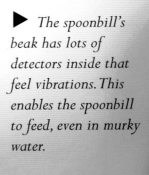

▶ *The spoonbill's beak has lots of detectors inside that feel vibrations. This enables the spoonbill to feed, even in murky water.*

Secretary bird

The secretary bird lives in Africa. It appears on the coat of arms, or state emblem, of Sudan and South Africa. The bird has an unusual habit—it stamps hard on grassy **tussocks** with its feet. This scares any small lizards, **mammals**, birds, or grasshoppers that may be hiding there. As they run away, the secretary bird stamps on them to stun or squash them. Then it tears them apart using its hooked beak.

◀ *The secretary bird has long, skinny legs like a* **wading bird**, *and a body like an eagle.*

Sun bittern

The sun bittern is found in Central and South America. The adult birds perform a special "broken wing" trick to protect their nest. If a predator approaches, the sun bittern will drag one wing along the ground as if it is broken. The predator will follow the apparently injured bird, thinking it will be easy to catch.

▶ *When the sun bittern is scared, it raises its wings to show off two large eye spots. The "eyes" make the bird's body look like the head of a much bigger, scarier animal.*

Foul fact!

Spoonbill chicks sometimes die from starvation while their parents take too long looking for food.

Spoonbills

Spoonbills wade through shallow water, swinging their open bill from side to side in the water. If any small fish, insects, or **crustaceans** touch the inside of the bill, the bird snaps it shut!

Big mouth

Some birds, such as pelicans, have a huge mouth that they use to snap up large prey. Other birds use their mouth to alarm predators. The bird may suddenly open its mouth wide to startle its enemy.

▲ *If frightened, a tawny frogmouth opens its beak wide and shows its yellow throat, hoping to scare away predators.*

Tawny frogmouth

The tawny frogmouth lives in Australia. By day, it sits very still in trees and is difficult to spot. At night, it hunts for insects, which it may dig from the soil or catch while flying. The tawny frogmouth either beats its prey to death or swallows it whole.

Toucans

Toucans live in the rain forests of South America. They use their huge, colorful bills to pick fruit to eat. The length of the bill enables them to reach fruit on branches that are too small to take their weight. During the mating season, male and female toucans throw fruit at each other to attract a mate.

◀ *The toucan's large bill may put off predators, but it is not strong enough to be used as a weapon.*

Pelicans

Pelicans are water birds found on many of the world's coastlines. A large pouch hangs under their beak. They eat fish, frogs, and crustaceans, such as crabs and shrimps. Sometimes they also eat smaller birds.

▼ *Pelicans expand their throat pouch to scoop prey out of the water. They drain off the water before swallowing the prey.*

Foul fact!

In medieval times, it was thought that mother pelicans fed their young with their own blood when food was scarce.

Peculiar predators

Some birds have horrid hunting habits. They may beat or peck their prey to death, or even push it onto branches or rocks. One bird even drinks the blood of other birds.

▶ *Kookaburras have a loud call that sounds like hysterical laughter.*

Kookaburras

Kookaburras live in Australia, New Zealand, and New Guinea. They mainly eat insects, worms, and crustaceans, but sometimes vary their diet with small snakes, mammals, frogs, and birds. They pounce on their prey from a perch, bashing large victims against a branch or the ground.

Vampire finch

The vampire finch lives on Wolf Island in the **Galápagos**. It feeds on blood, which it gets by pecking at the feet and wings of other birds. It also eats the eggs of seabirds called boobies.

Foul fact!

The vampire finch rolls the newly laid eggs of other birds against a rock to break them open. It then feeds on the contents.

◀ *A vampire finch feeds on the blood of a larger bird.*

European bee-eater

The European bee-eater is a **migratory** bird. It spends winter in warm places such as Africa, north-west India, and Sri Lanka, and the summer in Europe. It eats bees, wasps, and hornets. Before eating, the bee-eater hits the insect against its perch to knock off the sting. In just one day, the European bee-eater eats as many as 250 bees.

◀ *European bee-eaters build burrow-like nests up to 5 feet (1.5 meters) long in banks or cliffs.*

Stinky birds

Some birds are known for causing a real stink! Whether it is the birds themselves, their eggs, or the mess they make with their feces, the smell can be really awful.

▲ *Giant petrels regurgitate foul-smelling oil into their gravel nests to keep predators at a distance.*

Giant petrels

Northern and southern giant petrels lay stinky eggs. It is believed that the eggs smell to put off predators. Even after 100 years in museum collections, the eggshells still smell. The body of the southern giant petrel has a strong, musky smell, too. It feeds mainly on dead seals and penguins, as well as krill and squid.

Foul fact!

Starling guano is acidic and can damage buildings made of sandstone.

Hoopoes

Hoopoes are found in Europe, Asia, and Africa. The hoopoe makes a foul-smelling nest in a hole in a tree trunk or wall. It adds lots of feces to the nest to put off predators. It also squirts feces at intruders.

▶ *The Hoopoe eats insects and worms. It has a colorful crest, which it raises when excited.*

Starlings

Starlings are very common in the United Kingdom, where there are about 500,000 breeding pairs. The birds nest in spring, often in walls or attics. This can be a problem for homeowners, as the birds make lots of noise—and produce lots of guano. The feces are not only smelly, but can also carry diseases.

◀ *In winter, thousands of migrant starlings arrive in the United Kingdom from eastern Europe. They stay there for the winter.*

Beastly bats

Many bats look very strange. Humans have made up stories about bats being evil because of the way they look. But they actually do a lot of good, eating large numbers of harmful insects.

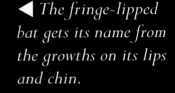

◄ *The fringe-lipped bat gets its name from the growths on its lips and chin.*

Fringe-lipped bat

The fringe-lipped bat lives in Central and South America. It eats insects, other bats, and frogs. Just by listening to the frogs' mating calls, the bat can tell which frogs are poisonous and which are safe to eat.

Wrinkle-faced bat

The wrinkle-faced bat lives from southern Mexico to Venezuela. It has lots of hairless folds of skin on its face. The bat roosts in trees by day. After dusk, it eats fruit such as ripe bananas.

◄ *When roosting, the bat pulls up a fold of skin from its chin and hooks it over the top of its head, covering its ears.*

Spectral bat

The spectral bat is one of the largest bats in the world. It has a wingspan of up to 3 feet (one meter). It is found in southern Mexico, Ecuador, Peru, Brazil, Guyana, Suriname, and Trinidad. The spectral bat hunts at night for birds, small mammals, reptiles, frogs, large insects, and fruit—and even other bats! Both parents take care of the single baby that is born each year. The father bat often sleeps with both the mother and baby wrapped in its wings.

Foul fact!

A spectral bat suddenly drops from a tree onto its prey as the prey passes below.

▲ *The spectral bat has long canine teeth. When it hunts, it drops onto its prey from above.*

Poisonous flyers

Some birds have developed an unusual protection against predators. They use poison in their feathers or skin to keep themselves safe from enemies.

▶ *The pitohui may be brightly colored as a warning to predators that it is poisonous.*

Pitohuis

Pitohuis are songbirds from New Guinea. These birds have high levels of poison in their feathers and skin, and smaller amounts in their bodies. They eat a type of beetle that contains the poison. The poison may protect the birds from predators and **parasites**.

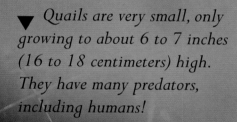

▼ *Quails are very small, only growing to about 6 to 7 inches (16 to 18 centimeters) high. They have many predators, including humans!*

Quails

Some European and **Eurasian** quails are poisonous, but not all of them and not all of the time. People who have eaten quail in northern Algeria, southern France, Greece, north-eastern Turkey, and Russia have been known to suffer vomiting, breathing problems, pain, and even **paralysis**.

Blue-capped ifrita

The blue-capped ifrita is a small, insect-eating bird found in New Guinea. It eats choresine beetles, which contain a poison. The poison is carried in the bird's blood, and is laid down in its skin and feathers. This protects it from predators.

◀ *The feathers of the blue-capped ifrita are beautiful, but dangerous to touch.*

Foul fact!

The poison in the feathers of ifritas is the same poison as that found in poison-dart frogs.

Make it!

Create your own vicious vampire bat and hang it from your bedroom ceiling. It will scare off unwanted visitors!

✄ *You will need:*

Thin paper or tracing paper
Black card
Paper clip
Black trash sack

Sticky tape
Newspaper
Two twigs
PVA glue
White card
Glitter glue
Black thread

1 Trace the half-bat shape below, using thin paper or tracing paper. Cut out the shape.

2 Fold the black card in half. Clip your tracing paper bat shape to the card. Line up the straight edge of the bat's body with the folded edge of the black card. Cut out the bat shape from the black card and unfold it to reveal a whole bat.

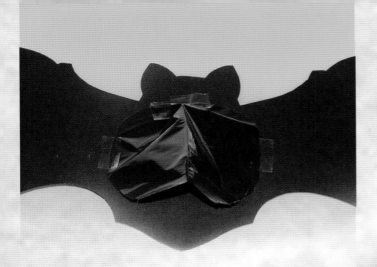

3 Cut out a circle of black plastic from the rubbish bag. Tape the circle to the body, leaving a gap to stuff the body with crumpled newspaper. Stuff and then seal with tape.

4 Glue twigs to the wing shapes to look like the bat's bones.

5 Cut a piece of black card to make a face. Stick the face onto the body as shown. Cut fangs from the white card and stick them to the face. Use glitter glue to make some sparkly eyes.

6 Stick some black thread to your bat and hang it up.

29

Glossary

Bacteria

Very small organisms, living things, that are found everywhere. Some bacteria cause illnesses, such as stomach upsets.

Carcass

The body of a dead animal.

Carrion

The dead or decaying flesh of an animal.

Crustacean

A type of animal that has a hard outer shell. They live in water, such as crabs, shrimps, or lobsters, or on land, such as wood lice.

Dabbling duck

Shallow-water ducks, including shovelers, that feed by bobbing forward and under the water so as to feed off the bottom.

Disgorge

To force something up from the stomach and out through the mouth.

Eurasian

Of or relating to Eurasia, the land mass formed by Europe and Asia.

Feces

Waste matter that passes out from an animal's anus as droppings.

Ferment

To make a substance change chemically from one state to another. When vegetation ferments inside a bird, it is broken down by living substances, such as yeast or bacteria, into a different state.

Filter-feeding

Animals that feed by straining or filtering tiny food particles from water. Flamingoes are filter-feeders. They squeeze water out through hairy attachments on their beaks, and eat the food particles that are left behind.

Galápagos

A small group of islands in the Pacific Ocean. They are part of the South American country of Ecuador.

Gizzard

Part of the digestive system of some birds, reptiles and fish. It is part of the stomach and has strong, muscular walls used for grinding up food.

Guano

The name given to the feces of birds, bats, and seals. It is often used as a fertilizer to help plants grow.

Krill

Krill are like tiny shrimps. They are eaten by crabeater seals, baleen whales, manta rays, and a few seabirds.

Lemmings

Small rodents that look similar to hamsters. They live in or near the Arctic, the cold region surrounding the North Pole.

Mammal

Warm-blooded animals with backbones and hair. They produce live young, not eggs. There are around 5400 species of mammals, ranging from the huge blue whale to the tiny bumblebee bat.

Migratory

When animals migrate, they move from one place to another, usually as the seasons change and food becomes scarce.

Nectar

A sugary liquid produced by plants. Some birds, such as hummingbirds, drink nectar. As they do so, they pollinate the plants that make the nectar, and this enables the plants to produce new seeds.

Paralysis

The condition of being unable to move.

Parasite

An organism that lives on or inside another organism, called a host. The parasite feeds off the host.

Poison-dart frogs

Poison-dart frogs are tiny, colorful, highly poisonous frogs. They are the only animals that can kill a human by touch alone.

Predators

Creatures that hunt and kill other animals.

Quarry

A hunted animal.

Regurgitate

To bring food back into the mouth after it has been swallowed.

Roost

When birds and bats roost, they rest or sleep. A roost is also the place, such as a tree branch, where birds and bats sleep.

Scavenger

A scavenger hunts for and eats dead animals, or carrion. Vultures and hyenas are scavengers. They feed on the bodies of animals that have been killed by predators.

Species

A group of animals that shares characteristics. Animals of the same species can breed with each other.

Tussocks

Clumps or tufts of growing grass.

Vermin

Small animals or insects that are harmful and are often difficult to control.

Wading bird

A long-legged shore bird, such as a sandpiper or curlew.

Wingspan

The distance from one wing-tip of a bird or bat to the other.

Index